Write your name.

Daniel

KiNg

Whenever Snake is scared or frightened he makes himself into an s shape and hisses *sssssss*.

S s

s
s
s
s
s
s

Action: Weave hand in an s shape, like a snake, and say *sssssss*.

Keep inside the snakes. Daniel

S S S S S S S S S S S S

S S S S S S S S

S S S S S S S S S S S S

S

S

S

Capital

S S S S S S

A a

The ants have found a picnic. Some of the ants crawl up the arm of a girl. She looks down and says *a, a, a, ants.*

Action: Wiggle fingers above elbow as if ants crawling on you, saying *a,a,a,a.*

Follow the ants to reach the ant hill.

Capital

5

T t

Some children are playing tennis.
They hit the ball to each other, *t, t, t, t.*

Action: Turn head from side to side as if watching tennis and say *t, t, t, t.*

Follow the bouncing ball.

Capital

I i

Inky Mouse got her name because she was covered in ink when she escaped from her cage.

Action: Pretend to be a mouse by wriggling fingers at end of nose and squeak *i, i, i, i.*

Follow the Inky paws to find Inky.

Capital

It is Bee's birthday. Inky has made a pink pig party cake with 3 candles to puff out *p, p, p.*

P p

Action: Pretend to puff out candles and say *p, p, p.*

Take the path to the pig's house.

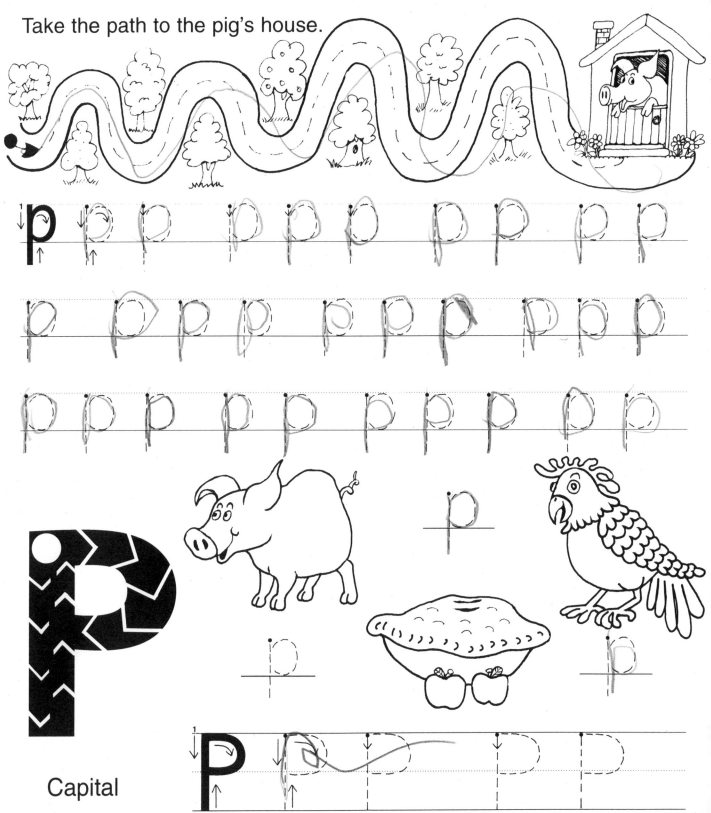

Capital

N n

Inky is woken up by a nasty noise. There is a model plane flying about going *nnnnnnnnnn*.

Action: Hold arms out at side, as if a plane, and say *nnnnnnnnnn*.

Help the robin to his nest.

Capital

Make each pair of snakes the same.

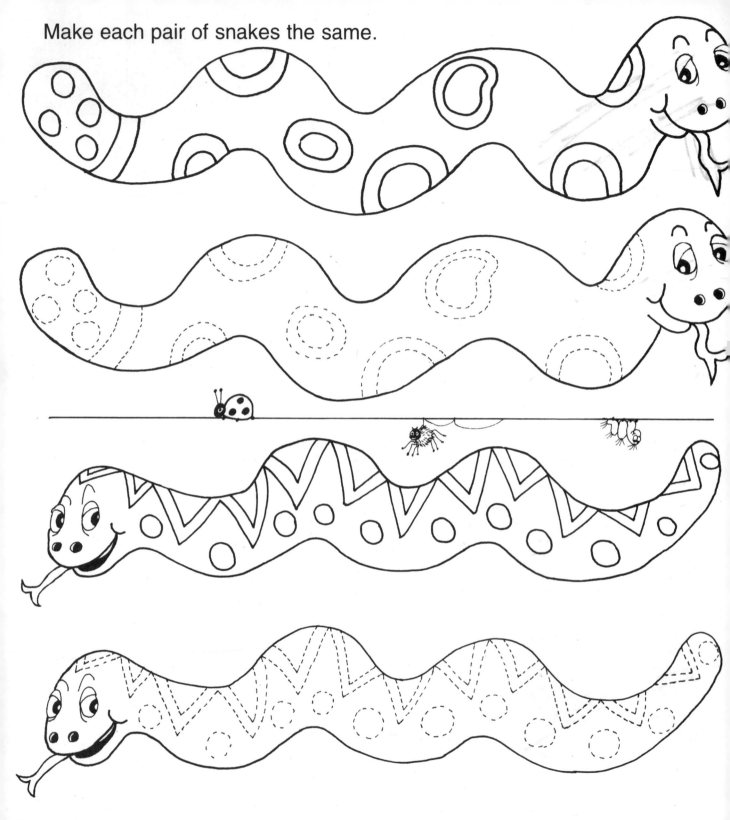

Join each
picture to its
beginning
sound.

a

i

p

s

n

t

15

Follow the trails

Write the first sound under each picture.

Put the feathers
on the parrots.

Practice of the u shape.

18

spy which things begin with the same sound.

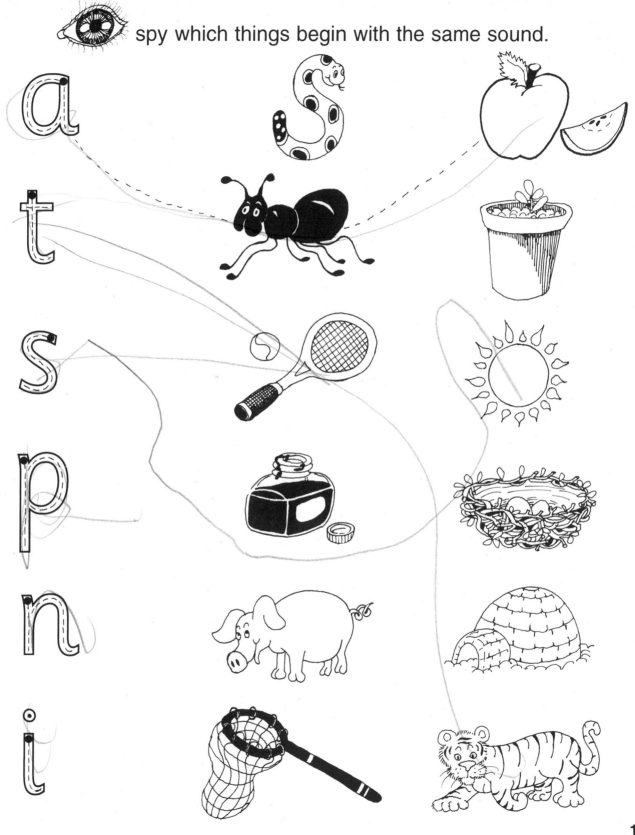

Some more writing practice.
Can you think of something that begins with each sound?

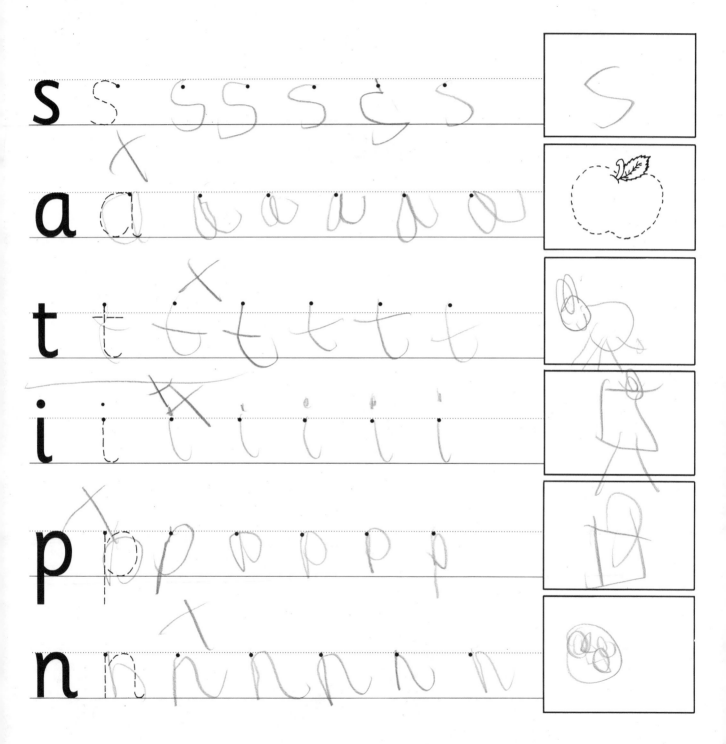

s

a

t

i

p

n

Match the capitals to the small letters.

A n

s

P

p I t N

T a i S

Write the words. Make sure you start on the dot.
Read them. Say each letter sound in turn and listen for the word.

at

in

it

sat

pin

pit

tin

pat

sit

The sounds must be said quickly
to hear the word. Say the first
sound slightly louder.

22

Numbers need correct formation, just as letters do.
(Workbook 1 - Number 1)

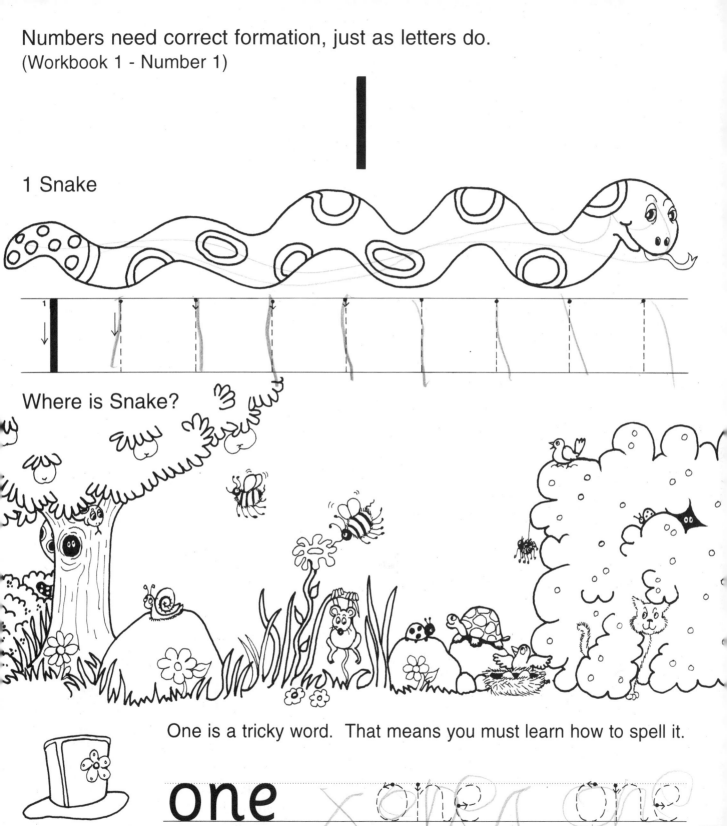

1 Snake

Where is Snake?

One is a tricky word. That means you must learn how to spell it.

one

Activity

Make your own sound book.

On a piece of paper, draw a curled up snake. Paint or draw in, then cut round to make him uncurl.

Hang him up.

Inky Pictures.

Put some ink or paint on one half of a piece of paper. Fold in half and press down.

Open up the paper and look at the ink. Sometimes it can be made into a picture.